Original title:
Potting Mix Musings

Copyright © 2025 Creative Arts Management OÜ
All rights reserved.

Author: Tobias Winslow
ISBN HARDBACK: 978-1-80581-780-2
ISBN PAPERBACK: 978-1-80581-307-1
ISBN EBOOK: 978-1-80581-780-2

Rhythms of Richness

In a bag of brown, I take a dive,
Worms meeting roots, oh how they jive!
Mysteries of mulch in every clump,
Is that a bug, or just a lump?

Digging deep, I hear them sing,
Planting joy in spring's warm spring.
With laughter blooms, I often tease,
Who knew dirt could bring such ease?

The Seedling's Saga

A tiny sprout with dreams so grand,
Wonders what it's like to stand.
"Do I need food, or sunshine bright?"
As I ponder, it takes flight.

Dancing roots in gentle breeze,
"This soil's magic, oh yes, please!"
With every inch, it shouts with glee,
"Watch out world, there's more of me!"

Reflections in the Garden

A garden mirror, muddy hue,
What do you see? Oh, that can't be true!
Bees buzzing loud, they strut and hum,
While plants just laugh in their own drum.

With every leaf, a tale to tell,
Of sunlight kisses and raindrop spells.
So grab a hoe, let laughter swell,
In our green world, all is well!

Earthy Epiphanies

Among the pots, my thoughts take flight,
A gardening guru, what a sight!
With my trowel, I dig for gold,
Turns out it's just marigolds, bold!

From plants we learn to never rush,
Let life unfold in a gentle hush.
Even weeds can be friends, I say,
At least they brighten up the day!

Sprouts of Inspiration

In the garden where dreams abide,
I planted seeds, just a little wide.
They sprouted up, oh what a sight,
One looked like a cat, it gave me a fright.

The tomatoes are gossiping over tea,
While carrots boast of their history.
But lettuce, alas, is such a tease,
Waving green fingers in the summer breeze.

Layers of Life

Digging deep in my garden bed,
Found a worm that looked quite well-fed.
He wiggled and wormed, it seemed so sly,
As if he fancied himself the next big spy.

On top, the daisies danced in delight,
Throwing shadows, what a lovely sight.
But beneath it all, chaos reigns near,
The turnips are plotting, oh dear, oh dear!

Sowing Stories

Every seed holds a tale untold,
From whispered dreams to laughter bold.
I sowed some beans, they stretched so tall,
Accusing the peas of trying to sprawl.

The sunflowers gossip about the moon,
Claiming they take her light all too soon.
While radishes roll their eyes in shame,
Oh, what a ruckus, this gardening game!

A Symphony of Soil

A concerto of roots underground,
Where every plant plays a funny sound.
The basil hums a fragrant tune,
While the cabbage sways like a dancing cartoon.

In harmony, they twist and sway,
Composing melodies in their own way.
But here comes the weeding, oh what a fuss,
They're not fans of the gardener's trusty bus!

Ebb and Flow of Growth

In a bag I find, so rich and deep,
A concoction of secrets, where dreams do seep.
Worms wiggle around, with a smile so wide,
In this earthy dance, they take it all in stride.

Seeds are sown, a quirky parade,
I wonder who's in charge of this botanical charade?
Sprouts stretch their arms, doing yoga at dawn,
While I sip my coffee, pondering the lawn.

The sun gives a wink, and the rain starts to giggle,
Plants in their pots take turns to wiggle.
A beetle declares he's king of the clover,
As I chuckle at greens, both timid and bold.

With watering cans clanging, I play the role,
Of head gardener here, with a heart and a soul.
So, here's to the mix, with all its delight,
In this garden of humor, I'm never uptight.

Fostering Flora

In the corner pot, a cactus stands proud,
While daisies gossip, a colorful crowd.
The herbs in their jars, they plot and conspire,
To create some chaos, a mischievous fire.

Roses roll their eyes, so dramatic and bright,
As violets whisper, "Is that a new height?"
Succulents cheer, "Look at us thrive!"
While I keep watering, hoping they'll survive.

A dandelion dreams of a five-star review,
"Best weed in the yard!" is its ambition too.
Tomatoes throw shade, "Aren't we divine?"
While peas just giggle, "We're tougher than thyme!"

I laugh with my plants, they're my silly crew,
Each pot tells a story, a life that's brand new.
Fostering life in this humorous way,
In a world full of green, let's dance and play!

In the Hands of Nature

I planted seeds with great delight,
But forgot to check the sun's good light.
Now my veggies grow with weeds in tow,
The salad's thick but lacks a glow.

A spider spun a web nearby,
Inviting friends who quickly fly.
My garden's now a social scene,
With bugs debating what's obscene.

Blossoming Ideas

I thought I'd grow a flower patch,
But all I got was quite a hatch!
The daisies danced with silly glee,
While dandelions escaped free.

Now ideas sprout in every row,
A garden filled with dreams to sow.
I'll take my shovel, make a mess,
Perhaps I'll find success, no less!

Woven Roots

Among the pots my thoughts entwine,
With tangled roots that laugh at time.
Each plant a dream, some wild and free,
But here I am, still sipping tea!

The neighbor's cat stalks through the vines,
As if to claim the secret signs.
With paws of mischief, she makes her mark,
Turning my garden into a lark.

Tangled in Green

My basil grows with such a flair,
While lettuce plots and schemes to pair.
A comedy of plants unfolds,
As they exchange their whispered holds.

Oh, thyme and rosemary have a chat,
Debating who's the coolest cat.
In this garden of clever schemes,
I giggle at my leafy dreams.

The Nurturer's Lament

In the garden of life, my back starts to ache,
I dig through the dirt for a delicate sake.
The plants all demand, yet I'm losing my cheer,
Why do they grow, while I sit here in fear?

With trowel in hand and soil on my face,
My flowers look bright, but my thoughts are a race.
I hear them all whisper, 'You could use a break!'
But I keep on planting for growth's sake, for growth's sake.

Cradled in Compost

In layers of mulch, my secrets reside,
A cabbage once whispered, now rots from inside.
The earthworms all snicker, they know all my woes,
While I dream of veggies that nobody grows.

The rich scent of soil, a perfume divine,
Yet my hands bear the proof of a hard life's design.
I chuckle at beetles who bubble and dance,
As I wrestle with weeds, not giving them a chance.

Nature's Rich Palette

Colors so vivid, in pots they all bloom,
Yet I trip on my hose, and I'm met with the gloom.
I swear that my daisies have mocked me today,
As I slip on my dreams, in the mulch where they play.

Can roses really be red? Not in my plot,
They've taken a turn, oh my, not a lot!
I laugh with the critters, a jester in green,
Nature provides, but I'm caught in between.

The Grounded Heart

Stuck in the muck, where my heart likes to roam,
I ponder the daisies and think of my home.
With laughter and soil bound tight in my soul,
The joys of the green keep me feeling whole.

Between every sprout and the weeds that I fight,
I'm crafting my dreams, in the warm morning light.
My heart may be grounded, but watch it take flight,
As I dance with the earth, in the magical night.

Nature's Palette

In a bag so brown and fair,
Worms gossip, unaware.
Seeds giggle at their fate,
Dreaming of a garden date.

Nutrients dance, all in line,
Whispering, 'Dirt, you're divine!'
Rain drops join the silly crew,
Splashing hopes of greenish hue.

Roots tickle, say, 'Not so fast!'
They pull along the comical cast.
With every sprout, a chuckle grows,
While the weeds plot mischievous woes.

Sun's shining, not a care in sight,
Plants swaying, what a silly delight!
They paint the world with leafy cheer,
In this green circus, laughter is near.

The Texture of Growth

There's a dance of grains so fine,
Each one plays its role in line.
A little clump says, 'Not today!'
While dust bunnies start a play.

Fingers dive into the mix,
Feeling all the nature's tricks.
A clod remarks, 'What a thrill!
If I could talk, I'd rhyme and spiel!'

Seeds boast, 'We'll outshine the rest!'
As neighbors tease, 'We're still the best!'
Digging deep, the laughter spreads,
As tiny sprouts tease all the heads.

With each layer, humor's unearthed,
In this soil, joy is birthed.
A pot of giggles, what a sight,
Plants strutting, oh so bright!

Earthbound Yearnings

Sunflowers stretch, what a view!
As daisies hum, they yell, 'Woohoo!'
The soil sighs, a grounding sigh,
While little roots dream to fly.

In pots of dreams, the herbs all scheme,
Basil shouts, 'I'll become a theme!'
Thyme replies, with a playful nudge,
'Let's grow taller, let's not budge!'

Moisture whispers, 'Stay awhile!'
While plants flash their biggest smile.
A little droplet says, 'Let's roll!'
As fungi conga, feeling whole.

Earth is laughing, dirt's in style,
Seeds chuckle, 'Let's run a mile!'
From potted dreams to garden beds,
The world blooms up, and joy spreads.

Garden of Whimsy

In the garden, mischief brews,
Pots converse with quirky views.
A cactus says, 'I'm feeling spiky!'
While daisies dance, so sprightly wily.

Roses giggle, 'We're so refined!'
But thorns tease back, 'No peace you'll find!'
Beetles jive, spinning in place,
Addicted to this garden grace.

The soil laughs, 'What a fine creation!'
With every sprout, a new sensation.
In the sunlight, shadows play,
Making merry in their ballet.

Whimsy reigns where green things grow,
With no end to the lively show.
Each plant whispers their own tale,
In this garden, joy prevails!

Sprouts and Sentiments

In tiny pots, hope takes root,
A sprout emerges, oh what a hoot!
With leaves that dance in the sun's bright glare,
It's the funniest plant, without a care.

Water spills, and dirt's a mess,
Yet laughter emerges, I must confess.
The garden's a stage, plants are the jest,
Each bloom and bud, nature's best quest.

The Ground Beneath

The ground below holds secrets deep,
Where worms compose, and secrets creep.
With roots that wiggle, the flowers sing,
Who knew dirt could be such a playful thing?

First, my seedlings poked their heads,
Then jumped to life, like silly threads.
They wiggle and giggle, oh what delight,
In the dance of soil, they take flight!

Fertilized Thoughts

Compost piles whisper their funky lore,
With every whiff, I laugh even more.
Eager earthworms join in the fun,
Turning leftovers into a gardening run.

The chicken poop, a potent blend,
Stirs up laughter I can't quite fend.
Fertilizer dreams take root and sprout,
Funny how growth brings that giggle about.

The Art of Care

With a gentle touch, I tend my greens,
Like a proud parent with wild daydreams.
A sprinkle of water, a dash of love,
They wiggle with joy, like a hand in a glove.

I chatter away to my leafy friends,
Sharing my woes that never seem to end.
Each leaf responds with a flirty sway,
In the comedy of nurture, who needs a play?

Fertile Imaginations

There once was a seed, so spry,
Dreamed of reaching the sky.
It plotted and planned,
With a watering can in hand.

But it tripped on a root, oh dear!
And whispered, "This is my fear!"
Yet laughter ensued,
As it squirmed in the dude.

With sunshine overhead, it danced,
In the dirt, it took a chance.
Imagining brussels in sight,
Oh what a silly delight!

In the end, it's not quite the food,
But a story of joy and a mood.
Seeds giggle while they grow,
In the garden's funny show.

Harvesting Hopes

In the garden, a carrot did grin,
"Pull me up and let the fun begin!"
With a tug and a pull,
Out it came with a cull.

Potatoes were hiding with flair,
"Guess my size if you dare!"
They laughed in the dirt,
"Make sure not to hurt!"

Tomatoes rolled in a race,
"Catch me quick— I'm a fast-paced!"
Yet they slipped through the cracks,
In a game of green snacks.

As we gather the crop, full of dreams,
Laughter bubbles and giggles like streams.
For it's not just the yield that we prize,
But the silly surprises in our eyes.

Nature's Notebook

In the soil, I found a pen,
Scratching notes with a tiny grin.
My compost is my plot,
With dirt-pretty thoughts, a lot!

Worms wiggle with the ink so blue,
Scribbling bits of what they do.
They send a note to the leaves,
"Don't forget the weed thieves!"

With daisies writing in soft curls,
They pen love songs for the swirls.
Bees buzzing in haiku form,
"Sweet honey, that's the norm!"

Every bud a story to tell,
Of how gardens grow so well.
Nature's notebook filled with cheer,
Bringing giggles every year.

Weaving with Weeds

Weeds stitch secrets in the ground,
With tangled threads all around.
They giggle and hide,
In the soil, they confide.

"Watch out! Here comes the rake!"
They tumble and twist, what a shake!
With dandelion fluff, they play:
"Where's the breeze? Let's fly away!"

Thistles don crowns, oh so grand,
Holding court in their green band.
While clover spins yarns of lore,
Each leaf holds a giggling score.

So let's toast to weeds, dear friend,
With laughter that never has to end.
For in all that's wild and untamed,
Funny stories are often acclaimed.

Whispers from the Earth

In the dark, where secrets dwell,
The whispers of roots start to tell.
A worm once dreamed of becoming a fly,
But settled for digging, oh my, oh my!

Tiny bugs crowd for a chat,
Discussing the joys of a warm welcome mat.
While shadows dance on the muddy floor,
The leaves spin tales of what's in store.

Raccoons debate if it's time for a snack,
While the critters munch on a well-trimmed track.
"Let's grow bigger!" the daisies declare,
As they stretch and wiggle without a care.

Each seed a wish on a soil-spun spree,
What marvels arise from just mud and glee!
So let's raise a glass to what's underground,
Where laughter and dirt twirled all around.

The Ground Beneath My Dreams

The soil's a sponge for the wildest schemes,
Where daisies plot and the grassline gleams.
"Should I be tall or just stay quite small?"
As blades of grass opine, they bicker and brawl.

A daffodil whispers to a stone so grand,
"Why do you sit there? Come lend me a hand!"
While critters perform their best circus acts,
Dancing through dirt in their joyful pacts.

A potato burrows, thinks it's a star,
"Next big movie? I'm raising the bar!"
While comets of seeds shoot across the field,
"Hold onto your hats! That's a wild yield!"

Dreams take root where the giggles grow,
The earth is alive with a comical flow.
Let's spread out wide and gather some cheer,
For the ground beneath dreams is always near.

Nurtured by Nature

A cactus wonders why it's so prickly,
While others tease it; "It's just a bit sickly!"
The pansies giggle, holding their ground,
"Let's start a show, let the humor abound!"

A tiny sprout feels the sun's warm embrace,
"Do plants feel joy, or is it a race?"
While clouds drift past with a mischievous laugh,
The trees join in for a leafy photograph.

Compost is swaying, oh what a sight,
"Here comes the lettuce, it's feeling quite bright!"
And the garden gnomes giggle in delight,
As they keep watch on the fun through the night.

So here's to the blossoms who grow with a grin,
And the roots that twirl as they spin and spin.
Nurtured by nature, they flourish anew,
With laughter and love, fresh as the dew.

Blooming Contemplations

Roses discuss their shade of the day,
"Should we go blush or brighter, I say!"
While daisies joke about taller blooms,
"Can't you just see us in theater costumes?"

Lettuce throws shade, in jest, on the night,
"Why not dress up, let's get it just right!"
And right then a breeze whispers silly songs,
As petals sway gently, where all belong.

A sunflower thinks it's the sun's best friend,
"Won't you come over? Let's just pretend!"
While the marigolds throw a funky parade,
A colorful jaunt in their sun-drenched charade.

So if you pass by where the blossoms conspire,
Just join in their laughter, if you feel inspired.
For blooming contemplations, they hold so dear,
Are sprinkled with humor and just a bit of cheer!

Nature's Canvas

In a world of dirt and leaves,
Each seedling dreams and weaves.
With worms that dance in total glee,
They plot a grand horticultural spree.

A trowel's friend, the garden spade,
Laughing as the sunlight fades.
The daisies blush at tulip jokes,
While artichokes promote their folks.

The grasshoppers hop like they know the score,
While daisies bloom, always wanting more.
A crow caws loudly, a poet's muse,
While carrots grumble about their views.

So here in nature's palette we create,
With a sprinkle of humor, it's never too late.
For soil and laughter together entwine,
In this garden of joy, everything's fine.

Layers of Life

In the layers of earth, we find delight,
Compost bubbling, a funky sight.
Worms wiggle down with no sense of time,
While radishes giggle, thinking they're prime.

With a sprinkle of water, the antics begin,
As sprouts peek out, where to begin?
Tomatoes tickle peas in a jolly jest,
While beets roll over, feeling quite blessed.

Mulch wears a crown, made of old grass,
Declaring to all, "I've got class!"
The daisies tease the fussy weeds,
"Join our dance, forget your needs!"

And when the sun sets, the laughter remains,
Nature's green humor forever sustains.
Layers of life, so vibrant and true,
In this place of growth, there's room for you.

The Alchemy of Soil

In the cauldron of earth, a witch's delight,
Mixing the magic, both day and night.
Fungi giggle, secrets they share,
While roots dig deep without a care.

A sprinkle of this, a dash of that,
Mushrooms forming their funky hat.
With nutrients dancing like they're on show,
Plants on the rise, putting on a glow.

A garden gnome winks as he tends the plot,
Whispering tales that can't be bought.
The sun beats down, a mischievous grin,
As lettuce jumps in a leafy spin.

In this concoction of nature's brew,
Every bump and root tells a story anew.
From a handful of dirt, we summon a crop,
In the alchemy of soil, we giggle and pop.

Sprouting Insights

Tiny shoots reaching for the sky,
Wondering if they'll ever fly.
With a wink from pebbles, they take their stand,
Learning quickly—this is quite grand!

A sunflower blinks, "Aren't I the best?"
While violets hum, taking a rest.
Chickadees chuckle at the goofy trees,
While roots collaborate like friends at ease.

In the patch, all wisdom grows,
With giggles hidden beneath cropped rows.
What's the secret to blooming bright?
Just be yourself and hold on tight!

So here we grow, with each sprouting leaf,
A garden of laughter, joy, and belief.
With insights sprouting like flowers in spring,
We find the funny in everything!

Nature's Classroom

In the garden, lessons grow,
Worms with wisdom in tow.
Rabbits think they own the patch,
While butterflies just love to hatch.

Noses buried in the earth,
Finding treasures of great worth.
Ants consult on what to do,
While snails take naps, just me and you.

Daisies prompt a silly dance,
While bees buzz in a merry trance.
All around, the sun shines bright,
Teaching us to relish light.

So here we learn, my friend,
That nature's lessons will not end.
Grab your spade and join the fun,
In this classroom, we are one.

Roots of Resilience

Beneath the soil, the magic spreads,
With quirky roots, not just in beds.
Dandelions sprout without a care,
While weeds just giggle, unaware.

In storms that rattle leaves up high,
Roots tug tight, they won't say goodbye.
Twisting 'round, a noble fight,
To show the world they hold on tight.

"Oh no!" the gardener starts to pout,
As garlic greens start to sprout.
But give it time, don't you fret,
Resilience is the safest bet.

So let us raise a glass today,
To all the roots that find their way.
In the garden of life, how they strive,
With laughter, love, they'll always thrive.

Quietude in the Garden

In a quiet nook where petals glow,
A squirrel shares secrets, soft and low.
Leaves whisper stories of summers past,
While time moves slowly, shadows cast.

Frogs play hopscotch on lily pads,
While nearby chatty chickadees laugh.
A garden gnome gives a knowing grin,
Watching chaos, where do we begin?

Breezes carry scents so sweet,
As the daisies sway, don't miss a beat.
With every twig and rustling sound,
Life finds joy in the peace around.

So join the frenzy, shake off the stress,
In this quietude, we find the best.
Nature giggles in hushed delight,
In the garden, everything feels right.

The Essence Beneath

Beneath the surface, stories wait,
Where tiny critters celebrate.
Roots host parties in the dark,
While earthworms wiggle, making their mark.

What's that smell? A mystery fair,
Compost stews with love and care.
Potatoes hide in a cozy nook,
While radishes peek from their nook.

Every trowel holds a tale,
Of muddy steps and joyous trails.
With a hearty laugh and a spade in hand,
Let's dig deep, it's quite grand!

So raise a glass to what we find,
The fun beneath, not far behind.
In the earth's embrace, we all partake,
Of life's sweet essence, make no mistake.

Essence of Earth

In bags they come, a treasure so deep,
Worms giggle softly, while playing their keep.
A sprinkle of humor, a scoop of delight,
Mixing and mingling, it feels just right.

Just add some water, watch wonders unfold,
The flowers are gossips, their secrets retold.
A dance of the roots, in soil they play,
Whispers of growth in a comical way.

A dash of this, a pinch of that,
The plants overhear where the garden's at.
With a wiggle and jiggle, they claim their space,
Tiny green stalks with smiles on their face.

So kneel in the dirt, embrace the good cheer,
Life's messy and muddy; we should all persevere.
As laughter erupts from this earthy brigade,
In the joy of planting, bright futures are made.

Tangents in the Dirt

In the depths of the garden, where secrets reside,
A potato's adventure would surely confide.
It dreams of the sky, while stuck underground,
Cracking up worms with each wiggle and sound.

Beans take a leap, reaching for stars,
While cabbage debates life and count its scars.
Then daisies burst out with giggles galore,
As they tickle the roots beneath compost's floor.

The carrots conspire to outgrow their kin,
While radishes shout, "Come on, join in!"
Together they plot, without fear or doubt,
A raucous revolution that's sprouting about.

So take a swift glance at this lively parade,
Where laughter's the currency, tossed freely, unweighed.
In the tangents of dirt, each plant plays a part,
In a hilariously chaotic, green work of art.

Illuminated by the Sun

Sunshine's a joker, it beams with a grin,
As seedlings stretch upward, their new lives begin.
With every warm ray, they waltz on the ground,
In a spunky ballet, so joyous, unbound.

The sunflowers salute, as the daisies do spin,
While broccoli's brooding, with a smirk on its chin.
Carrots, oh carrots, they're giddy with glee,
In their underground burrows, what a sight to see!

Tomatoes are gossiping, ripening quick,
While peppers try dodging the silly old tick.
With nectar and nonsense, they sip on the light,
In this quirky assembly, all feels just right.

So laugh with the plants as they soak in the fun,
In a world where the garden and humor have spun.
With roots that are dancing, and leaves in a whirl,
Every day blossoms, a comical pearl.

The Meditative Earth

In the stillness of soil, where silence can creep,
The earth shares its wisdom while taking a leap.
A zen garden giggles, where daisies unwind,
While wise old oak trees share jokes of their kind.

The beetroot confesses with underground tales,
As worms join the chorus, crossing leafy trails.
Moss folds in laughter, a carpet of green,
In this peaceful retreat, a comical scene.

The daisies find yoga, stretching so wide,
While pansies wear sunglasses, taking it in stride.
Together they bloom, in sublime unity,
Proclaiming that laughter brings harmony.

So breathe in the earth, its humor and grace,
Celebrate the giggles in this special place.
For in every patch, a funny life's worth,
Is woven through roots in the meditative earth.

Fertile Dreams

In a bag of dirt, I found my dreams,
Worms are swimming in their schemes.
Potatoes wearing muddy shoes,
Planting hopes and growing blues.

Each seed a laugh, each sprout a joke,
Garden gnomes around us poke.
The daisies dance, the tulips twirl,
In this messy, leafy whirl.

Nature's jesters, all so spry,
Compost piles that touch the sky.
With every rake and shovel's swing,
The garden giggles, what joy they bring.

Fertile earth, where punchlines grow,
With each new bloom, our laughter flows.
Beneath the sun, with dirt-stained hands,
Life is funny in these lands.

The Heart of the Garden

In the heart of green, where veggies bloom,
Radishes grow in a jolly room.
Carrots whisper funny tales,
While peppers don their joke-telling veils.

The squash are juggling, what a sight!
Cucumbers laugh till the fall of night.
Tomatoes roll and shout with glee,
In the garden's joyful jubilee.

Sunflowers strut like they own the place,
With goofy grins and leafy grace.
Insects buzz their silly songs,
While plants sway to the rhythm of throngs.

Every weed, a punchline missed,
Yet laughter thrives through morning mist.
With every turn and silly twist,
The heart of the garden can't be missed.

Seeds of Reflection

Seeds of laughter tucked away,
Sprouting smiles in bright array.
A daisy winks, a dandelion giggles,
With belly laughs, the garden wiggles.

As I plant these little dreams,
Morning dew adds silver streams.
Reflecting on the dirt and fun,
Each tiny seed shines like the sun.

I trowel through the thoughts that sprout,
Digging deep to pull them out.
In this patch of earth, I find,
A world of humor intertwined.

With every sprig, a memory sown,
In nature's whispers, I've grown.
Seeds of reflection, laughter's hail,
In every bloom, the joy prevails.

Digging Deep

Digging deep in soil so rich,
Found a worm who made a stitch.
With every shovel, laughter steeps,
In this treasure where nature peeps.

Beneath the roots, a dance unfolds,
Cabbages prance, their story told.
While beetles bust a funny move,
In this garden groove, we all approve.

Roses blush as they giggle shy,
While carrots plot amidst the sighs.
As nature sways, the humor blooms,
In the cozy embrace of earthen rooms.

So here I dig with joy and cheer,
Gathering chuckles, we've all come near.
In the depths of dirt, where laughter's steep,
Life's funny finds, as I dig deep.

Troweling Emotion

With a trowel in hand, I dig my woes,
Planting my dreams where the sunlight glows.
Mix in a chuckle, a pinch of despair,
As I bury my worries beneath the soil's care.

The spade in my grip feels like a wand,
Weaving spells of green, of grass and fond.
Each scoop's a giggle, each clump a muse,
Who knew such a hobby could lighten my blues?

In the dirt, I find my life's little quirks,
Sifting through life like it's all just perks.
Shovel a bit and let laughter sprout,
Planting joy's seeds, there's no room for doubt.

So with every weed pulled, a grin appears,
I grow my own funny, watering with cheers.
Nature's my therapist, no need for a chat,
Just tell me your secrets, I'll plant them like that!

The Pulse of Planting

As I plant these seeds, I feel a beat,
The rhythm of nature, oh what a treat!
Sowing silliness, I chuckle and grin,
With every little green, a new joke begins.

I'm a gardener now, life's jester supreme,
Digging up punchlines, living the dream.
Sprinkling laughter like it's magic dust,
Watch out for gags, in soil we trust.

With worms as my minions, they wriggle and squirm,
Turning my troubles into a new term.
Each sprout is a laugh, each bloom a jest,
In the garden of humor, I feel truly blessed.

So let's raise our spades, and don't be shy,
Plant a few giggles, let worries go by.
In the great outdoors, let's have our fun,
For each little seed, there's a new pun begun!

Cultivating Calm

In the garden's embrace, I find my peace,
Weeding out worries, they tend to cease.
With every soft shovel, a chuckle I sow,
Calm in the chaos, watch my laughter grow.

Tending to thyme, with a wink and a smile,
Every herb tells stories, stay for a while.
They sprinkle my life with aromas so fine,
Mixing calm with comedy, all in due time.

Sunshine and laughter go hand in hand,
My garden's a stage, nature's own band.
The daisies are giggling, the petunias sigh,
In this patch of delight, let's reach for the sky.

With soil on my hands and joy in my heart,
Cultivating calm, I play my sweet part.
As I water the blooms, I can't help but beam,
Life's silly moments, like flowers, they gleam!

Harmonies of Humus

In the depths of the dirt, where the laughter hums,
I hear the sweet chorus of all the fun dums.
Worms wiggling happily, singing a tune,
While the daisies dance gently beneath the moon.

Building my garden with giggles galore,
Composting joys right outside my door.
Layer upon layer, my humor's the key,
In this earthy symphony, I'm wild and free.

Oh, the melodies swirl as I mix and I mound,
Creating my masterpiece, where laughter is found.
With every small sprout, a new jest takes flight,
In the garden of glee, everything feels right.

So join in the chorus, we'll laugh and we'll grow,
In the warm soil of humor, let our spirits flow.
From humus to happiness, let's harmonize loud,
In this funny little garden, we stand so proud!

The Hum of Harvest

In the garden beds, I muse,
With dirt-smudged hands and laughter too.
The worms beneath, they wiggle and giggle,
As I question what makes plants grow biggle.

Sunshine beams, a dance with dew,
Each sprout a joke, who knew they grew?
I talk to blooms, they nod and sway,
Whispering secrets in their leafy play.

In this patch of green, I seek my crown,
With every weed, I root 'em down.
A banter with beets, I tip my hat,
As radishes argue, 'We're far too fat!'

Harvest time comes with a comedic twist,
A squash that rolls, I can't resist.
The funniest garden I've ever seen,
Where veggies giggle and grass is green.

Earthy Epiphanies

Digging deep, I find the truth,
In leafy whispers, return to youth.
Compost tales, a funny refrain,
When lettuce plays hide and seek with rain.

Worms wear glasses, a sight indeed,
Pondering life as they munch on seed.
Fertilizer jokes, it's quite a stretch,
But nothing beats a well-made sketch!

Beans in lines, they start to prance,
They say, 'Hey there! Join the dance!'
While carrots chuckle, buried below,
'The deeper you dig, the funnier the show!'

In earthy realms, I find delight,
Where blooms share laughter every night.
Underneath the soil, wisdom creeps,
Unpacking laughter while the garden sleeps.

Fertility of the Mind

Planting ideas in the fertile ground,
Watch them grow as they spin around.
Thoughts sprout like peas, just out of sight,
Who knew my brain was so full of light?

A row of dreams in neat little rows,
Weeding out doubts as self-confidence grows.
The broccoli whispers, 'Don't take it hard,
Just keep it fresh, we'll be your backyard.'

Cabbage debates on what's next to sow,
While zucchini giggles, 'Not yet, you know!'
In this garden of whims, ideas take flight,
As laughter takes root beneath the moonlight.

With every thought, I feed the soil,
Finding humor in each daily toil.
The fruits of my mind are sweet and ripe,
In a plot of giggles, I just type!

Composting Conversations

Gather around for a humorous chat,
Where scraps of my lunch all sit like a mat.
Banana peels giggle, saying they're wise,
'Compost us gently, we open your eyes!'

Old bread and leaves share a raucous jest,
'We're here for a party, not just a rest!'
Eggshells chime in, 'We're fragile but bold,
With nutrients gleaming, we break from the mold.'

While coffee grounds snicker, 'We give such a boost,
To plants intertwining, we're really the juice!'
An assembly of scraps with stories to tell,
In the belly of soil, they all cast their spell.

In this funny mix, the cycle is clear,
Laughter and life blend, never a drear.
From trash to treasure, the dance goes on,
In composting circles, it's never all gone.

Reflections in the Garden

In the garden, plants converse,
They gossip soft, oh what a curse!
One leaf boasts of its new green wear,
While petals giggle, without a care.

The weeds join in, a raucous crew,
They claim the soil, oh what a view!
A dandelion claims it's grand,
While daisies roll their eyes, not planned.

The sun winks down, a cheeky spark,
As shadows dance, their own little lark.
A moonflower whispers through the night,
"Oh, look at me, I'm quite the sight!"

Oh, nature's play, a silly scene,
With watering cans and leaves so green.
In this plot, antics reign supreme,
Garden life, a funny dream!

The Poetry of Planting

Digging deep, the shovels sing,
As worms do a wiggly thing.
Seeds tumble into beds of earth,
Dreaming of a flower's rebirth.

The carrots whisper, 'We're underground!'
While peppers jabber, 'Oh, we're renowned!'
Tomatoes claim they're the real stars,
While squash rolls in, with its great cars.

Watering cans, a sloshing rhyme,
Each droplet sings of summer's prime.
A sunflower waves, "Look at my height!"
While tiny blooms wish they'd take flight.

When harvest comes, a joyous dance,
Vegetables twirl, they take a chance.
So here we plant with grins on our face,
In this silly, green-fingered place!

Soil's Silent Secrets

Underneath, the critters plot,
With roots that tangle in a knot.
A mole chuckles, "No one can see!"
While ants march proudly, full of glee.

Each crumb of dirt, a tale to tell,
Of dandelions that dared to rebel.
The fungi whisper, "We own this ground!"
While lilies laugh at their leafy crown.

The rain taps lightly, a gentle beat,
As mud pies form at garden's feet.
With splashes, puddles start to gleam,
Nature's mischief—a muddy dream!

So here we dig with secret smiles,
Reading the soil's fun-filled files.
In every clump, a hidden jest,
In dirt and laughs, we find our rest!

In the Embrace of Earth

Beneath the sky, we sow delight,
With pots and plants, our hearts take flight.
A gnome stands guard, wearing his hat,
As squirrels plot just where they're at.

The herbs conspire with fragrant cheer,
While radishes blush, skin so dear.
"A sprinkle of love, and look at us grow!"
The garden hums, its own lively show.

As bugs join in, a waltz ensues,
The leaves quiver with laughter's muse.
A ladybug winks, "I'm quite the dame!"
While each bend of stem, plays a game.

In this haven, joy intertwines,
As sun and shade sing in designs.
With dirt on hands and smiles so wide,
In the earth's embrace, we take our stride!

Soil Symphony

Beneath the dirt, a ruckus thrives,
Worms are dancing, doing high-fives.
Roots are jamming, singing tunes,
While grubs hum softly, under the moons.

Compost chefs stir with glee,
Mixing flavors; oh, can't you see?
Dry leaves rattle, twigs snap tight,
It's a concert in the cool moonlight.

Fungi strum on ancient lyres,
Tickling moss, igniting fires.
Beetles tap their tiny feet,
In this earthy beat, life is sweet.

So grab your shovels, let's all play,
In this garden groove, we'll sway away!
Join the chorus of the ground,
Where nature's humor can be found.

The Language of Loam

In the quiet of the garden bed,
Gossip travels! - as it is said.
The chubby moles, they know it all,
Sharing tales of who will fall.

The daisies giggle, the sunflowers beam,
While snails plot mischief—oh, what a scheme!
The roots whisper secrets in the night,
Under silver stars, it's quite a sight.

Mulch mutters softly, cutting in,
Saying, 'You're the compost king!'
Every scoop tells a story tale,
In this loamy language, we prevail.

So let's decode this earthy chatter,
Where the tiniest bugs, they truly matter.
A cacophony beneath our feet,
In this dark world, life is sweet.

Nature's Nurture

The sun winks down with a golden smile,
Water droplets dance for just a while.
In the pot as plants sway and wiggle,
The earth drops riddles, oh just giggle.

Seeds have dreams hidden in their shell,
To sprout and bloom, oh can't you tell?
But pesky weeds whisper sly and fast,
"Step aside, we're here to last!"

But nature's plan is mighty clear,
With sunshine, rain, and a dash of cheer.
Plants stand tall, reaching for the sky,
While bugs conspire, plotting, oh my!

With every layer of dirt and clay,
Life's a party, come what may!
In this garden of joy, we all play,
Nature's nurture rules the day.

Underneath the Surface

Beneath the surface, chaos reigns,
The whole underground crowd, it entertains.
Ladybugs gossip, ants march in lines,
While beetles boast of their nightly designs.

Gravelly rocks tap dance with glee,
As roots and worms create a spree.
Earthy friends chuckle, sharing a laugh,
Oversized squash finds the tiniest path.

In this hub of roots, life's a feast,
But oh, beware of the hungry beast!
With each passing day, there's more to see,
Popping up sprouts as funny as can be.

So join the fun, dig in with zest,
Underneath the surface, life's at its best!
In this garden gala, we frolic and cheer,
Where every dirt clod brings us near.

Gardening Green: A Reflection

My plants are chatty, don't you know?
They whisper secrets to the hoe.
The weeds are plotting, it's quite absurd,
They scheme with worms, oh how they stirred!

I caught a slug trying to sneak a bite,
He thinks he's sly, but he's outta sight.
With every seed I bravely sow,
I think of all the things to grow!

My garden gnome's a bit aloof,
He never jokes, that stubborn goof.
I told him once to take a peek,
He shrugged and said, "I'm just a freak!"

But still I laugh, my heart is light,
With dirt on hands, I feel just right.
Each bloom a chuckle in the sun,
In this great garden, we have fun!

Cultivating the Soul

With shovels raised, we dig away,
In search of things that love to play.
A cat in boots, a frog in hat,
Turns out my yard's a fancy spat!

The carrots dance, the radishes spin,
The lettuce giggles, saying, "Let's begin!"
Neighbors stop by, they laugh aloud,
Who knew my patch could draw a crowd?

I talk to daisies, they talk back,
They tease my shovel, "It's gone slack!"
Compost dreams mixed with oil junk,
A garden party with all its funk!

The skies may frown, the rains may pour,
But joy erupts from every spore.
With every hoe and spade I wield,
I cultivate the laughs revealed!

Trowel and Tonic

In the shed, my trowel's on the shelf,
Chillin' out, enjoying itself.
A spade's gone rogue, the rake's in jest,
They bicker 'bout which tool's the best!

I mix some dirt with laughter, true,
Toss in some seeds, sprinkle on dew.
The plants all giggle in the breeze,
"Oh please, not more garden chores, we're trees!"

A watering can sings out loud,
While flowers blush, feeling proud.
The greenhouse blooms with comic grace,
It's like we've won a gardening race!

Muddied feet and sun-kissed face,
Among my greens, I've found my place.
With every bloom, a funny glance,
In this wild, whimsical garden dance!

Seeds of Serenity

I plant my thoughts in cozy pots,
Expecting blooms, but getting knots!
A sunflower said, "Why so glum?"
I shrugged and said, "It's just a con!"

The basil's gossip keeps me sane,
While zucchinis plot their great campaign.
I swear I saw my corn doing jazz,
While peas just snoozed, content to razz.

A cheeky squirrel stole my hat,
He wore it well, that little brat!
The flowers blushed a rosy hue,
When he made jokes, as squirrels do!

Yet here I sit with dirt on knees,
As laughter floats upon the breeze.
In every seed, a story stored,
In nature's space, I'm never bored!

Digging for Answers

In the garden, I take a chance,
With a trowel tight in my grip,
Digging deep like a curious clown,
What lies beneath? A lost old flip-flop!

Worms wiggle, they give me a stare,
As I wonder if they have a clue,
'What's in the dirt?' I quip and ponder,
Maybe treasures, or just last week's stew.

Seeds sprout up in a wild whirlwind,
While gophers giggle from their burrowed lair,
I throw my hands up and laugh to the sky,
Who knew digging could lead to such flair?

So I shovel on, my thoughts in a twist,
Every scoop tells a story, I insist,
If soil could speak, oh what tales it'd weave,
Of pesky weeds and a garden that grieves.

Beauty Buried Beneath

Under the surface, magic does wait,
Planting dreams, or perhaps, a tin plate,
A carrot? A rock? Who knows what I'd find,
Beauty's buried, but the dirt's unkind!

Potatoes hide like shy little kids,
While I poke and prod with all of my bids,
'Will they grow bigger than last year's feast?'
I chuckle at roots turning into a beast.

The sun shines down on this messy domain,
A patch of earth where I feel quite insane,
Yelling to daisies, "You'd better take flight!"
As the weeds wrangle all through the night.

But each sprinkle of hope brings laughter anew,
As herbs tease my nose with a fresh morning dew,
Oh what a riot, this gardening spree,
In this chaotic world, I'm completely free!

The Dance of Dirt

In the garden, I spin a wild jig,
As soil flings up like a mischievous pig,
Each trowel poke is a dance so spry,
I twirl with daisies, oh my oh my!

Mud squelches under my carefree feet,
In this earthy ballet, who's missing the beat?
Rabbits join in, with a hop and a dash,
Throwing down veggies in a boisterous splash.

My flowers are swaying, though winds are quite bold,
The basil is laughing, its story retold,
As sunflowers rock like they're at a grand show,
Who knew dirt dancing would steal the whole show?

Step, plant, repeat, the groove goes on,
With every new sprout, my worries are gone,
So to the rhythm of worms and sweet bees,
I dance through my garden, so wild and at ease!

Enchanted Garden Whispers

Amidst petals whispering soft little dreams,
The garden hums with its quirky themes,
'Tis the tulips who giggle at the nearby bees,
While ivy tries tickling the knees of the trees.

When peeking at gnomes, I swear they conspire,
Plotting how best to outsmart the gardener's fire,
With shades of green, they gather and scheme,
While daisies burst forth with a laugh and a beam.

Potting soil warbles in a thick, muddy tongue,
It holds all the secrets of old folk and young,
In this enchanted place where no rule exists,
I chat with the onions — too funny to resist.

So come take a stroll through this wild leafy maze,
Where flowers exchange the most curious praise,
In the heart of the earth, with a grin wide and bright,
The garden's enchanted, it twinkles all night.

Whispered Roots

In the dark of my pot, oh what a chat,
Roots gossip below, 'Look! There's a rat!'
They twist and they turn, oh what a scene,
In their earthy playground, who knows what they mean!

With a trowel in hand, I dig and I poke,
Each scoop is a mystery, a jolly good joke.
'What's this? A worm! Slithered and sly,'
'He says he's a gardener, just passing by.'

Oh, the seedlings are nervous, they wiggle and shake,
'Is that a raindrop? Or a big mistake?'
As I water my dreams, they giggle and sway,
In the potting world, humor leads the way!

So here's to the roots, with their whimsical chats,
In a world full of dirt, we laugh like old cats.
With each little sprout, more giggles arise,
In this garden of banter, there's joy in disguise!

Blooming Thoughts

In my little green patch, the flowers conspire,
Each bloom holds a secret, a petty desire.
'What if we danced, beneath the sun's rays?'
They twirl and they shimmy, in flowery frays!

The daisies debate who's the fairest of all,
'It's me!' said the tulip, standing so tall.
But the violets giggle, 'Let's not be mean,
With colors so vibrant, it's a flower routine!'

While petals are primping, the weeds start to plot,
'Let's sneak through the cracks and take over the lot!'
But the flowers just chuckle, 'Good luck with that plan,
We'll trample those weeds, we're a flower-power clan!'

So here in this garden, where laughter takes root,
With petals and petals, we dance and we hoot.
For in nature's embrace, joy's always a must,
Let's bloom in the laughter, in each colorful gust!

Clay and Contemplation

Sitting in mud, what can I say?
The clay offers wisdom in its own way.
'Could I be an artist? Or just a big lump?'
It sighed with a chuckle, 'A glorious hump!'

With hands in the soil, I ponder my fate,
Am I sculpting a garden, or tempting a trait?
The gnomes on my shelf wink, 'You're doing just fine,'
We're all a bit silly, sipping on sunshine!

Do I create a new world with flowers and art?
Or just reshape my worries, get rid of that part?
The clay seems to giggle, 'Just mold and just play,'
In this messy existence, find joy every day!

So here in the dirt, I embrace every thought,
With clay in my fingers, it's happiness fought.
Let humor abound in this muddy old place,
For in playful creation, we all find our grace!

Tilling the Mind

In my sandy backyard, I till with a grin,
What thoughts come to life? Where do I begin?
Every shovel of dirt brings laughter and grit,
It's a comedic journey, I can't seem to quit!

As I poke at the earth, worms start to cheer,
'Our party's in soil, come join us, my dear!'
With trowels as instruments, we play a grand tune,
Dancing with roots 'neath the bright glowing moon.

The rabbits all gossip, the frogs croak their rhymes,
In this quirky old garden, we've all got our times.
Each tilled patch is laughter, each seed a new joke,
In the life of our soil, together we poke!

So let's plant some merriment, water it well,
In this garden of joy, we all know the spell.
For in tilling the mind, with laughter so bright,
We cultivate happiness, from morning till night!

Whispers of the Wild

In garden beds where secrets sigh,
The gnomes play hide and seek by and by.
With trowels in hand, we make our stand,
Digging up dreams with a playful hand.

A worm gave a wink, what a sight!
He danced around in delight each night.
Planting with laughter, we take our time,
The daisies whisper, 'Is this a crime?'

Insects giggle when the sun is bright,
While bees and butterflies take their flight.
We sip our tea, share a joke or two,
The garden's alive, and so are you!

This patch of dirt is our happy place,
Where seedlings sprout with a little grace.
With every chuckle, the flowers bloom,
In this wild wonder, there's always room.

Seeds of Solitude

In lonely rows, the seedlings grow,
Each asking, 'Where's my buddy, though?'
A dandelion ponders with a frown,
'Why can't I just take the crown?'

A single sprout in a plot so bare,
Talks to a weed, says, 'Is life fair?'
They swap wild tales of rain and sun,
Finding humor in the job they've done.

The carrots whisper of a crunchy fate,
While busy bees don't hesitate.
'A party's coming, won't you see?'
But the shy seeds hide behind the tree.

Gardening's an art, so they sigh,
'But who'll hear our poems, oh my?'
Yet together they sprout, full of zest,
In solitude, finding joy, they're blessed.

The Buried Treasure

In the soil lies a mystery deep,
Where secrets slumber and roots do creep.
A rusty spoon, an old boot found,
Who knew diggers would abound!

Beneath the mulch, a treasure map,
With scribbles, giggles—what a flap!
'X' marks the spot where no one goes,
A hidden stash of garden woes.

Spades clash with laughter, digging wide,
As worms cheer on from inside.
'Another trinket!' we cry in glee,
What a find amongst the greenery!

And just like that, we strike gold twice,
Finding joy in these little vices.
So here's to dirt, to treasure chests,
The garden yields the very best.

Serpentines of Soil

The paths we tread are twisted and fun,
With crickets chirping, and laughter spun.
A twisty trail where the flowers jive,
Each step a dance, we're so alive!

The pebbles giggle 'neath our feet,
As snails in shells take a slow retreat.
'Shush,' says thyme, 'don't spoil the cheer!'
'The sun's our DJ, let's all draw near!'

Twisting and turning, the roots do play,
In our little wonderland, come what may.
With earthy whispers, we can't resist,
The soil's a friend, you get the gist!

So let's laugh with the worms in their dance,
And give the garden a twirl, a chance.
In the serpentines where the fun begins,
We find pure joy, in each other's grins.

Grounded Whispers

In the garden, I did toil,
With dirt that makes my fingers boil,
I added spice, a little thyme,
My indoor herbs declare it's prime.

The pot said, "I can't hold it all!"
I laughed as plant leaves chose to sprawl,
My basil dreamed of far-off lands,
While cilantro plotted with its hands.

Then came the squirrel with cheeky glee,
Dancing 'round the rosemary tree,
I shouted, "Hey, this is my patch!"
He winked, then made a quick dispatch.

With every sprout, I jest and cheer,
These leafy friends, they bring such cheer,
I talk to them, they giggle back,
In my soil world, there's no lack.

A Tapestry of Trowels

With trowels raised, we dig and play,
In the dirt, we shape our day,
A shovel here, a spade just right,
We plant our dreams in morning light.

Fertilizer jokes are quite a blast,
Who knew that compost made us gasp?
As worms debate about their fate,
We find our fortune on a plate.

The rake decided it was wise,
To share its wit 'neath cloudy skies,
"Why rake when you can let it be?"
I pondered, giggling esoterically.

So here we dance, with soil and grin,
In our patch, where fun begins,
With trowels in hand, we laugh and scheme,
In the garden, we live the dream.

Roots of Understanding

Beneath the surface, secrets lie,
Roots gossip as the days go by,
"Here comes the rain, let's hold a show!"
They tickle worms, put on a glow.

They argue 'bout the best sun spots,
And judge the human's flower pots,
"This one's shallow! That's too deep!"
While in the dirt, they dare to creep.

Fungi laugh at every plan,
Whispering truths that only they can,
"A little more mulch, a pinch of cheer,"
They toast their cups of root beer.

So beneath the chaos, life persists,
A root confab with playful twists,
With laughter shared in earthy hues,
We've learned the joys from nature's clues.

Sowing Serenity

With seeds in hand, I start to scheme,
A garden path, my dream supreme,
I toss them wide, they dance in air,
"Oh, they'll grow up, without a care!"

Each sprout's a joke, a funny jest,
They rise up tall as if to fest,
"I'm taller than the last of you!"
As beans and peas share their debut.

Sunflowers march, they strut with might,
While carrots giggle out of sight,
"You'll never find us, we're too cool!"
They chuckle back from garden school.

So here's the truth, a lesson learned,
In dirt and blooms, our laughter's earned,
Sowing seeds of joy and fun,
In nature's realm, we're ever one.

www.ingramcontent.com/pod-product-compliance
Lightning Source LLC
Chambersburg PA
CBHW070319120526
44590CB00017B/2744